WHEN I GROW UP

Taylor Swift

By **LEXI RYALS**

Illustrated by
ERWIN MADRID

Scholastic Inc.

No matter what happens in life, be good to people. Being good to people is a wonderful legacy to leave behind.

—T.S.

(Taylor Swift)

Photo Credits:

cover main: Ray Tamarra/Getty Images; cover background: chrispecoraro/iStockphoto; 1 background: Vanesa Djordjevic/Dreamstime; 3 frame: Dominik Pabis/iStockphoto; 3 background in frame: CG Textures; 5, 7 inset: Sean Pavone/Dreamstime; 7 main: Kajdi Szabolcs/ iStockphoto; 8 background: DigtialStorm/iStockphoto; 8 inset: PN_Photo/iStockphoto; 9 image background: JTGrafix/iStockphoto; 10–11 background: TheFunTimesGuide.com; 12: Pavel Losevsky/ Dreamstime; 13: Scholastic Inc.; 14: Al Messerschmidt/Getty Images; 15 background: R. Gino Santa Maria/Shutterfree, Llc/Dreamstime; 16: Scholastic Inc.; 17: Nati Harnik/AP Images; 18: Scholastic Inc.; 19: Frank Micelotta/Invision/AP Images; 21 top: Al Pereira/WireImage/Getty Images; 21 bottom: Marc Piasecki/FilmMagic/Getty Images; 23: Scholastic Inc.; 24 tv: GodfriedEdelman/iStockphoto; 24 SNL: Dana Edelson/NBC/NBCU Photo Bank via Getty Images; 25: Jason Merritt/Getty Images; 26 top left: Everett Collection/Shutterstock, Inc.; 26 top right: Kevork Djansezian/Getty Images; 26 bottom: Denise Truscello/WireImage/Getty Images; 27: Gareth Cattermole/TAS/Getty Images for TAS; 28–29: Alexpro9500/Dreamstime; 30: Greg Allen/Invision/AP; 31 top left: Bibigon/Thinkstock; 31 top right: StanRohrer/iStockphoto; 31 bottom left, 31 bottom right: Scholastic Inc.

This unauthorized biography was carefully researched to make sure it's accurate. Although the book is written to sound like Taylor Swift is speaking to the reader, these are not her actual statements.

ISBN 978-0-545-86261-5

Text and illustrations © 2015 by Scholastic Inc.

All rights reserved. Published by Scholastic Inc., *Publishers since 1920*. SCHOLASTIC and associated logos are trademarks and/or registered trademarks of Scholastic Inc.

10 9 8 7 6 5 4 3 2   15 16 17 18 19 20/0

Printed in the U.S.A   40

First printing, September 2015

Book design by Marissa Asuncion

My name is Taylor Swift. I was born on December 13, 1989, in Reading, Pennsylvania. I grew up in a small town nearby, called Wyomissing, on a Christmas tree farm with my parents and my younger brother, Austin. My mom ran the farm and my dad worked for a financial company.

I've known I wanted to be a country music star since I was six years old, when I got my very first country music **album**, *Blue*, by LeAnn Rimes. I listened to it over and over until I had memorized every song. My parents encouraged my dream by enrolling me in singing lessons.

Another dream of mine was to perform onstage, so my parents signed me up for acting lessons, too. I starred as Sandra Dee in a local production of the musical *Grease*. I also auditioned for different Broadway shows in New York City, which was only a train ride away from my hometown. But I never got any of the parts I auditioned for.

Back home, I began to focus more on music. I started singing **karaoke** at local fairs and festivals when I was ten years old. I won several contests and even got to open a hometown show for the Charlie Daniels Band, country music legends.

When I was eleven, I recorded my first **demo tape** of me singing my favorite country songs. My mom drove me down to Nashville, Tennessee, where many country music stars get their start, and I left my demo with all of the country **music labels**. Unfortunately, no one wanted to give me a **record deal** then. But I wasn't about to give up on my dream!

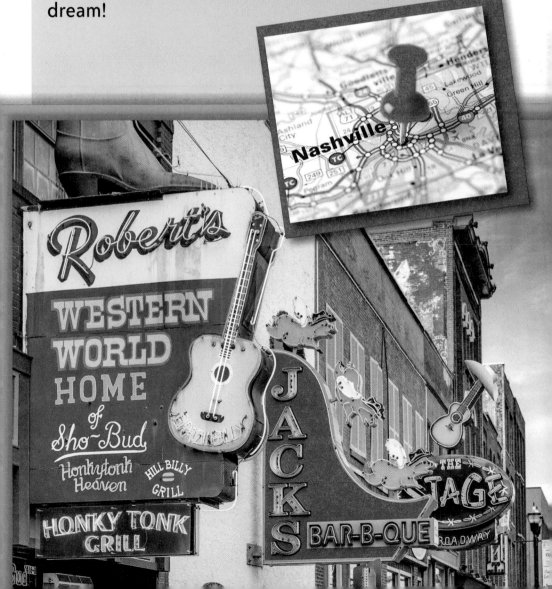

In sixth grade, my friends decided they didn't like me anymore. They left me out of the group and made fun of me. It was awful! I learned to play guitar that year and started writing songs. I always turned to music when I felt sad, and it made me feel better to write down how I was feeling. I wrote one of my very first songs about those mean girls. It's called "The Outside."

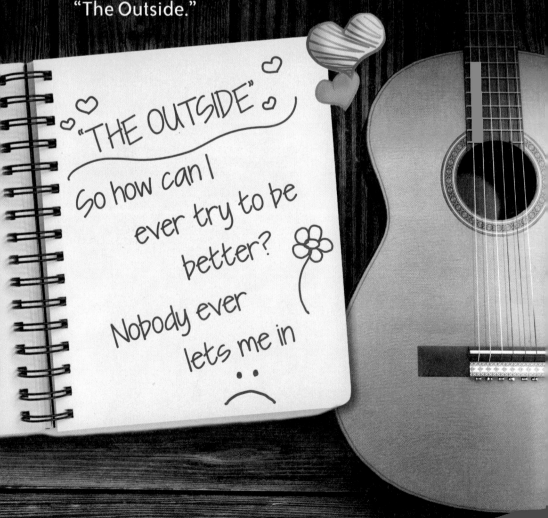

"THE OUTSIDE"

So how can I
ever try to be
better?

Nobody ever
lets me in

My family could see how serious I was about becoming a country music singer. I spent nearly all of my time writing songs, singing, practicing guitar, and performing whenever I could. When a music label offered me a **development deal**, my whole family moved with me to Nashville. They've always supported my music dreams!

Unfortunately, my development deal didn't work out. That company wasn't interested in letting me write my own songs, so I knew it wasn't a good fit. I was disappointed, but it only made me more determined to write great songs and find the right music label to work with.

★★★★★
I kept writing songs, and when I was fourteen, Sony offered me a job as a staff writer. I was the youngest writer they'd ever had! I worked with more experienced songwriters who helped me learn how to really express myself.

When I was sixteen, I finally signed a record deal, with Big Machine Records. I was so excited! Big Machine Records brought in some of the best **producers** in country music to help me record my first album, *Taylor Swift*. They gave me lots of guidance, but they also listened to what I wanted. Recording in a professional music studio was really fun, but it was also a ton of work to juggle with high school!

A lot of people didn't think a teenager should record an album. They said that no one would want to listen to songs about teenage problems. But my record label believed in me. Since I'd been writing songs for three years, I had a lot of material to choose from! I'd written about my ex-friends, my first boyfriend, and having a crush on a boy who didn't know I liked him. My music came from my heart, and the feelings I sang about were familiar to other teens like me.

uckily, lots of people (and not just teens) loved my music! Within a year, *Taylor Swift* went **platinum**. My first hit was "Tim McGraw," followed by "Teardrops on My Guitar." I got to go on tour as the opening act for different country music stars, including George Strait and Rascal Flatts. It was tough to balance music, high school, and friends, but it was worth it. I graduated with great grades, and I loved being on the road and getting to meet all of my new fans.

After that, I couldn't wait to record another album. My second album, *Fearless*, came out in 2008, when I was eighteen years old. I worked with other songwriters and producers, but I wrote most of the songs myself. Two of the most popular songs from *Fearless* were "Love Story" and "You Belong with Me." The album went platinum almost immediately—it was so cool! I went on a yearlong tour that took me all over the United States. It was my first time **headlining** a tour, and I had so much fun! I couldn't believe that my dreams of being a country music star were all coming true.

My third album, *Speak Now*, came out in 2010, when I was twenty-two years old. It debuted at number one and has sold over 6 million copies! This was the first time I'd written every song on an album all by myself, so it meant a lot to me. As usual, I wrote songs about things that had actually happened in my life, including "Back to December," which was an apology to an ex-boyfriend, and "Mean," which was my way of telling a music critic to stop bullying me.

I went on my *Speak Now* world tour for almost two years, playing huge arenas around the globe. I'd never had the opportunity to travel to so many amazing places, and I loved getting to see famous landmarks and try **exotic** foods. It was exhausting, but so much fun. Luckily, I was able to take breaks between different parts of the tour so that I could rest, spend time with friends and family, and get back into the recording studio to work on my next album.

Red was my fourth album, and it was all about love. I'd had my heart broken a few times by then, so I used those experiences to write many of the songs, like "I Knew You Were Trouble" and "We Are Never Ever Getting Back Together." I worked with songwriters who focused on pop and alternative styles, so it had less of a country sound than my earlier albums. Red debuted at number one in October 2012 and was my fourth album to be certified **quadruple platinum**. I guess my fans liked it!

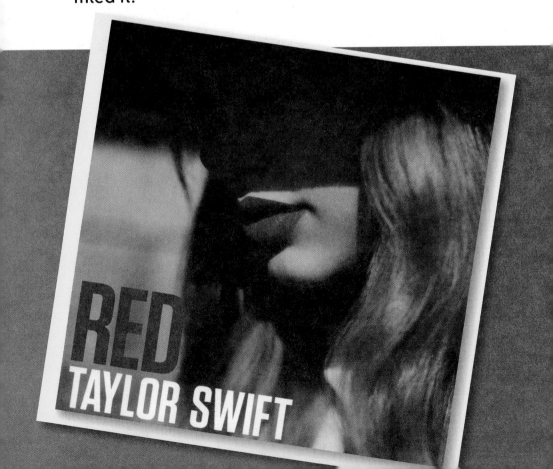

Later that year, I launched another worldwide tour to promote *Red* and was on the road for almost two years. In 2013, I won a very special award from the Country Music Association. It's called the Pinnacle Award, and it's given to artists who have reached great levels of success. Garth Brooks is the only other singer to ever win it. It was a huge honor, and it meant so much that I cried when they gave it to me!

After headlining huge tours, releasing multiple albums, and winning some big awards, I was officially a star. One downside to being famous is that the media pays a lot of attention to me. I get photographed everywhere I go, and there are a lot of articles written about what I'm wearing or who I'm dating. It's nice that my fans want to know all about me, but sometimes people say things that are untrue or that really hurt my feelings. Mostly, I try to ignore those stories and focus on my music and my fans.

My fans are the best part of being a star. I love meeting them at shows and events. But my favorite thing is to totally surprise a fan. For example, I went to a prom with one fan for a show on MTV. I also leave comments on fans' websites and blogs. One time, I took a car full of toys to a fan's home for her son after hearing she was having a hard time. I even photobombed a fan's family picture session in a Nashville park! Seeing the look on fans' faces when I surprise them is priceless. And getting to hear how my music has affected them means the world to me.

After four successful albums and three major tours, I decided it was time to change things up. I wrote a lot of new songs on the *Red* tour, and I realized that none of them were country songs. I was inspired by pop music and was ready to record my very first pop album! My record label wasn't sure if it was a good idea, but they trusted me. So I found the best pop songwriters and producers in the music industry and begged them to work with me. I spent most of 2014 writing, recording, and experimenting with my new sound—and it really paid off.

I released my fifth album, *1989*, in October 2014, and I was so nervous that I barely slept the night before it went on sale! I didn't have to be so worried, though, because my fans loved it. The album sold more than 1.2 million copies the first week it went on sale, making it my most successful release so far. Everyone embraced my new pop sound in songs like "Shake It Off" and "Blank Space." I am so glad that I trusted my instincts and tried something new. Fear should never hold you back from taking a risk!

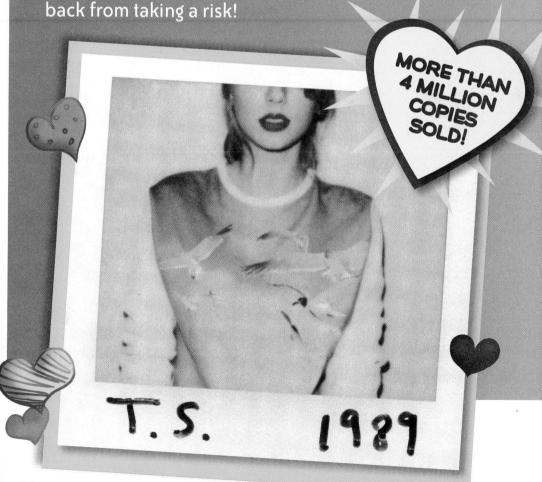

MORE THAN 4 MILLION COPIES SOLD!

T.S.   1989

My music career has given me the chance to do a lot of really cool things. I designed a clothing line that was sold nationwide. I've been the face of a makeup line and was in a commercial with a ton of supercute kittens! And I've released several of my own perfumes. I also appeared in concert movies for Miley Cyrus and the Jonas Brothers as well as in music videos for my friends Brad Paisley and Kellie Pickler.

I've also been able to try my hand at acting, which is so much fun! I've guest starred on *CSI: Crime Scene Investigation*, hosted *Saturday Night Live*, and had a **cameo** in the hit show *New Girl*. I had a small role in the movie *Valentine's Day* and played an animated character when I recorded the voice of Audrey in *The Lorax*. My biggest movie role so far has been Rosemary in *The Giver*, the 2014 film based on the bestselling novel.

It always feels great when other people love my music, and I feel honored each time I win a new award. So far, I've won seven Grammy Awards, sixteen American Music Awards, nine Country Music Association Awards, seven Academy of Country Music Awards, multiple Billboard Music Awards and Nashville Songwriters Association International Awards, and more!

I've spent a lot of time on tour since my career started, and I'll likely go on a lot more tours before my career is over. I've been lucky to have talented musicians tour with me, including Ed Sheeran, Florida Georgia Line, Neon Trees, Kellie Pickler, and even Justin Bieber. My favorite thing about being on tour is getting to meet my fans in so many different places and hear their stories. I try to meet as many as I can—even if it means signing autographs for hours!

I wanted my *1989* world tour to be really special and different from my previous tours. I had lots of new fans who love pop music, and I even had a new band for the occasion. Recently, I'd been inspired by Broadway shows, so I wanted my *1989* tour to have lots of big sets. I love surprising my audience whenever I can with special guests and new songs. I wanted this to be my best tour yet!

As much as I love being on the road, it's always nice to come home after a long trip. When I'm not working I like to spend time with my friends, family, and my two cats, Meredith Grey and Olivia Benson. My apartment in New York City is where I now spend most of my free time. I love staying in, eating take-out, baking cookies, and having dance parties with my best girlfriends. My other passions include reading, painting, and hunting for antiques.

So what's next for me? I plan to keep doing more of what I love: writing songs, recording music, touring, and working with other talented musicians. My job is better than I ever imagined it would be when I was a kid. I'm so thankful that I get to live out my dream by performing and making music every day, and I can't wait to see what the future will bring!

TIME LINE

DECEMBER 13, 1989:
I was born in Reading, Pennsylvania.

2000:
I started singing karaoke at fairs and festivals.

2002:
I learned how to play guitar and wrote my very first song, "The Outside."

2003:
I moved to Nashville with my family to pursue my dream of becoming a country music star.

2006:
I signed a record deal with Big Machine Records and recorded and released my first album, *Taylor Swift*.

2008:
I released my second album, *Fearless*.

2010:
I released my third album, *Speak Now*, and had a small role in the movie *Valentine's Day*.

2011:
I traveled all over the world on my *Speak Now* tour and recorded the voice of Audrey in *The Lorax* animated movie.

2012:
I released my fourth album, *Red*.

2014:
I starred in the film *The Giver* and released my fifth album, *1989*.

GLOSSARY

ALBUM: a long recording on a record, CD, or digital download that usually includes a set of songs

CAMEO: a small role in a movie, play, etc., that is performed by a well-known star

DEMO TAPE: a recording that shows what a performer can do

DEVELOPMENT DEAL: when a music label promises to develop a musician's skills and image before committing to recording an album

EXOTIC: from another part of the world

HEADLINING: being the main performer in a show or concert

KARAOKE: a form of entertainment in which people take turns singing popular songs into a microphone over prerecorded music

MUSIC LABEL: a company that produces musical recordings and represents musical artists and bands

PLATINUM: an award that is given to a singer or musical group for selling at least one million copies of a record

PRODUCER: someone who is in charge of making and usually providing the money for a play, movie, or record

QUADRUPLE PLATINUM: an award that is given to a singer or musical group for selling at least four million copies of a record

RECORD DEAL: a contract between a musician or band and a music label in which they agree to record and produce an album